I0528962

"This Day Thou Shalt Be With Me In Paradise."

(Luke 23:43)

Meditations on the Second Word from the Cross

Archbishop Fulton J. Sheen

Copyright © 2021 by Al Smith

Printed in the United States of America. All rights reserved.

Cover design by Janicka Barman
www.twitter.com/barman_janika

On the cover: Jesus and the Two Thieves (2008) painting by Michael D. O'Brien
© Michael D. O'Brien.

Scripture quotations are taken from the Douay-Rheims edition of the Old and New Testaments.

No part of this book may be reproduced, stored in a retrieval system, or transmitted in any form, or by any means, electronic, mechanical, photocopying, or otherwise, without the prior written permission of the publisher, except by a reviewer, who may quote brief passages in a review.

Bishop Sheen Today
280 John Street
Midland, Ontario, Canada
L4R 2J5

www.bishopsheentoday.com

Library of Congress Cataloging-in-Publication Data

Names: Sheen, Fulton J. (Fulton John), 1895-1979, author. | Smith, Al (Allan J.), editor. | Sheen, Fulton J. (Fulton John), 1895-1979. Cross and the Beatitudes. | Sheen, Fulton J. (Fulton John), 1895-1979. Rainbow of sorrow. | Sheen, Fulton J. (Fulton John), 1895-1979. Seven last words. | Sheen, Fulton J. (Fulton John), 1895-1979. Seven virtues. | Sheen, Fulton J. (Fulton John), 1895-1979. Seven words of Jesus and Mary. | Sheen, Fulton J. (Fulton John), 1895-1979. Seven words to the Cross. | Sheen, Fulton J. (Fulton John), 1895-1979. Victory over vice. | Sheen, Fulton J. (Fulton John), 1895-1979. Cross and the Beatitudes.

Title: This Day Thou Shalt Be With Me In Paradise: Meditations on the Second Word from the Cross / Archbishop Fulton J. Sheen: compiled by Al Smith.

Description: Midland, Ontario: Bishop Sheen Today Publishing, 2021. | Includes bibliographical references.

Identifiers:
paperback ISBN 978-1-999229-29-1
e-Book ISBN 978-1-990427-62-6
hardcover ISBN 978-1-990427-86-2

Subjects: LCSH: Jesus Christ — Seven last words.

Second Printing

J.M.J.

To Our Lady, Seat of Wisdom,
In Humble Petition That,
Through The Immaculate Heart Of Mary,
The World May Find Its Way Back To
The Sacred Heart of Jesus

Ad Maiorem Dei Gloriam
Inque Hominum Salutem

The Seven Last Words of Christ

The First Word

*"Father, Forgive Them For They
Know Not What They Do."*

The Second Word

"This Day Thou Shalt Be With Me In Paradise."

The Third Word

*"Woman, Behold Thy Son;
Behold Thy Mother."*

The Fourth Word

*"My God! My God! Why Hast
Thou Forsaken Me?"*

The Fifth Word

"I Thirst."

The Sixth Word

"It Is Finished."

The Seventh Word

*"Father, Into Thy Hands I
Commend My Spirit."*

Contents

Introduction

I have learned more from the
crucifix than from any book.

St. Thomas Aquinas

Archbishop Fulton J. Sheen was a man for all seasons. Over his lifetime, he spent himself for souls, transforming lives with the clear teaching of the truths of Christ and His Church through his books, his radio addresses, his lectures, his television series, and his many newspaper columns.

The topics of this much-sought-after lecturer ranged from the social concerns of the day to matters of faith and morals. With an easy and personable manner, Sheen could strike up a conversation on just about any subject, making numerous friends as well as converts.

During the 1930s and '40s, Fulton Sheen was the featured speaker on The Catholic Hour radio broadcast, and millions of listeners heard his radio addresses each week. His topics ranged from politics and the economy to philosophy and man's eternal pursuit of happiness.

Along with his weekly radio program, Sheen wrote dozens of books and pamphlets. One can safely say that through his writings, thousands of people changed their perspective about God and the Church. Sheen was quoted as saying, "There are not one hundred people in the United States who hate the Catholic Church, but there are millions who hate what they wrongly perceive the Catholic Church to be."

Possessing a burning zeal to dispel the myths about Our Lord and His Church, Sheen gave a series of powerful presentations on Christ's Passion and His seven last words from the Cross. As a Scripture scholar, Archbishop Sheen knew full well the power contained in preaching Christ crucified. With St. Paul, he could say, "For I decided to know nothing among you except Jesus Christ and him crucified" (1 Cor. 2:2).

During his last recorded Good Friday address in 1979, Archbishop Sheen spoke of having given this type of reflection on the subject of Christ's seven last words from the cross "for the fifty-eighth consecutive time." Whether from the young priest in Peoria, Illinois, the university professor in Washington, D.C., or the bishop in New York, Sheen's messages were sure to make an indelible mark on his listeners.

Given their importance and the impact they had on society, it seemed appropriate to bring together in this anthology some of Archbishop Sheen's meditations on the Seven Last Words Our Blessed Lord spoke from the Cross on Calvary.

The meditations contained in this book are taken from several books and articles written by Sheen between 1933 and 1945.

The Seven Last Words. (New York: Century, 1933)

The Seven Last Words and the Our Father. (Huntington, Indiana: Our Sunday Visitor 1935)

Calvary and the Mass. (New York: P. J. Kenedy and Sons,1936)

The Cross and the Beatitudes. (New York: P. J. Kenedy and Sons,1937)

The Rainbow of Sorrow. (New York: P. J. Kenedy and Sons, 1938)

Victory over Vice. (New York: P. J. Kenedy and Sons, 1939)

The Seven Virtues. (New York: P. J. Kenedy and Sons, 1940)

Seven Words to the Cross. (New York: P. J. Kenedy and Sons, 1944)

Seven Words of Jesus and Mary. (New York: P. J. Kenedy and Sons,1945)

These mediations have been selected to provide nine unique reflections for study and meditation on the Seven Last Words.

First Meditation - A reflection on the words spoken by Christ from the Cross.

Second Meditation – A reflection on a passage from the Lord's Prayer.

Third Meditation – A reflection on a part of the Mass.

Fourth Meditation – A reflection on one of the Beatitudes.

Fifth Meditation – A reflection about sorrow and suffering.

Sixth Meditation – A reflection addressing one of the seven deadly sins.

Seventh Meditation – A reflection on the virtues.

Eighth Meditation – A reflection on dealing with individuals who reject the Church and Christ's teachings.

Ninth Meditation – A reflection on the unity of Jesus and Mary.

As the reader ponders these reflections, they might have to pause for a moment or two over a sentence that is full of deep meaning that stirs the heart. He might also find that Archbishop Sheen has repeated certain lines throughout these reflections to drive home a point or an important theme, as any good teacher would do.

On October 2, 1979, when visiting St. Patrick's Cathedral in New York City, Pope John Paul II embraced Fulton Sheen and spoke into his ear a blessing and an affirmation. He said: "You have written and spoken well of the Lord Jesus Christ. You are a loyal son of the Church."

On the day Archbishop Sheen died (December 9, 1979), he was found in his private chapel before the Eucharist in the shadow of the cross. Archbishop Sheen was a man purified in the fires of love and by the wood of the Cross.

It is hoped that, upon reading these reflections, the reader will concur with the heartfelt affirmation given by St. John Paul II and countless others of

Sheen's wisdom and fidelity. May this writing by Archbishop Fulton J. Sheen evoke a greater love and appreciation for the Church, the Passion of Lord Jesus Christ, and the need for us to look into our souls each day.

Archbishop Sheen's dynamic personality combined with his brilliant mind, tireless pen, and eloquent voice has made him one of the best-known figures in the world. His radio and television appearances have been phenomenally successful and are still viewed today. His books and magazine articles continue to gratify and attract a boundless circle of readers. This collection of meditations gives still another example of why this continues to be so today.

First Meditation

This Day Thou Shalt Be With Me In Paradise

There is a legend to the effect that when, to escape the wrath of Herod, Saint Joseph and the Blessed Virgin were fleeing into Egypt with the Divine Child, they stopped at a desert inn. The Blessed Mother asked the lady of the inn for water in which to bathe the Babe. The lady then asked if she might not bathe her own child, who was suffering from leprosy, in the same waters in which the Divine Child had been immersed. Immediately upon touching those waters baptized with the Divine Presence, the child became whole. Her child advanced in age and grew to be a thief. He is Dismas, now hanging on the Cross at the right hand of Christ!

Whether the memory of the story his mother told him now came back to the thief and made him look kindly on Christ, we know not. It might have been that his first meeting with the Saviour was on the day when his heart was filled with compunction on hearing the story of a certain man who went down from Jerusalem to Jericho and fell among robbers. Perhaps, too, his first intimation that he was suffering with the Redeemer came to him as he turned his tortured head and read an inscription which bore His name, "Jesus";

His city, "Nazareth"; His crime, "King of the Jews." At any rate, enough dry fuel of the right kind gathers on the altar of his soul, and now a spark from the central Cross falls upon it, creating in it a glorious illumination of faith. He sees a Cross and adores a Throne; he sees a condemned Man, and invokes a King: "Lord, remember me when Thou shalt come into Thy Kingdom."

Our Blessed Lord was owned at last! Amidst the clamor of the raving crowd and the dismal universal hiss of sin, in all that delirium of man's revolt against God, no voice was lifted in praise and recognition except the voice of a man condemned. It was a cry of faith in Him whom everyone else had forsaken, and it was only the testimony of a thief. If the son of the widow of Nain, who had been raised from the dead, had cried out a word of faith in the Kingdom of One who was seemingly losing His Kingdom; if Peter, who on the Mount of Transfiguration had seen His face shine like the sun and His garments whiten like snow, had acknowledged Him; if the blind man of Jericho whose eyes were opened to the light of God's sunshine had been opened anew to proclaim His Divinity, we should not have been surprised. Why, if any of these had cried out, perhaps the timid disciples and friends would have rallied, perhaps the Scribes and Pharisees would have believed! But at that moment when death was upon Him, when defeat stared Him in the face, the only one outside the small group at the foot of the Cross to acknowledge Him as

Lord of a Kingdom, as the Captain of Souls, was a thief at the right hand of Christ.

At the very moment when the testimony of a thief was given, Our Blessed Lord was winning a greater victory than any life can win, and was exerting a greater energy than that which harnesses waterfalls; He was losing His life and saving a soul. And on that day when Herod and his whole court could not make Him speak, nor all the power of Jerusalem make Him step down from the Cross, nor the unjust accusations of a court-room force Him to break silence, nor a mob crying, "He saved others; Himself He cannot save," bring from His burning lips a retort, He turns to a quivering life beside Him, speaks, and saves a thief: "This day thou shalt be with Me in Paradise." No one before was ever the object of such a promise, not even Moses nor John, not even Magdalen nor Mary!

It was the thief's last prayer, perhaps also his first. He knocked once, sought once, asked once, dared everything and found everything. When our spirits stand with John on Patmos, we can see the white-stoled army in Heaven riding after the conquering Christ; when we stand with Luke on Calvary, we see the one who rode first in that procession. Christ, who was poor, died rich. His hands were nailed to a Cross and yet He unlocked the keys of Paradise and won a soul. His escort into Heaven was a thief. May we not say that the thief died a thief, for he stole Paradise?

Oh, what greater assurance is there in all the world of the mercy of God? Lost sheep, prodigal sons, broken Magdalens, penitent Peters, forgiven thieves! Such is the rosary of Divine forgiveness.

God is more anxious to save us than we are to save ourselves. There is a story told to the effect that one day Our Blessed Lord appeared to Saint Jerome, saying to him, "Jerome, what will you give Me?" Jerome answered, "I will give you my writings," to which Our Lord replied that it was not enough. "Then," said Jerome, "what shall I give you? My life of penance and mortification?" But the answer was, "Even that is not enough!" "What have I left to give Thee?" cried Jerome. Our Blessed Lord answered, "Jerome, you can give Me your sins."

PRAYER

DEAR Jesus! Your kindness to the penitent thief recalls the prophetic words of the Old Testament: "If your sins be as scarlet, they shall be made as white as snow: and if they be as red as crimson, they shall be white as wool." In Your words of forgiveness to the penitent thief, I understand now the meaning of your words: "I have not come to call the just, but sinners ... They that are in health need not a physician; but they that are ill." "There shall be joy in Heaven upon one sinner that doth penance more than upon ninety-nine just who need not penance." I see now why Peter was not made Thy first vicar on earth until after he had fallen three times, in order that the Church of which he was the head might forever understand forgiveness and pardon. Jesus, I begin to see that if I had never sinned, I never could call You "Saviour." The thief is not the only sinner. Here am I! But Thou art the only Saviour.

The Seven Last Words, 1933

Second Meditation

Hallowed Be Thy Name

"Hallowed be Thy Name"

"Amen, I say to thee, this day thou
shalt be with me in paradise."

God's name is hallowed by the recognition of His
power and glory. The thief recognized God's power
despite His powerlessness, and God's glory despite
His defeat.

Picture two scenes as this second word is being
spoken. On opposite sides of Sion, there were men
hanging on trees. On one side of the hill, Judas was
hanging from a tree; on the opposite side hung Our
Lord between two thieves. Note the difference in
attitude of Judas and the thief on the right. Both were
thieves. But there was this difference. Judas thought
God's glory was purely external, manifested by
earthly pomp and circumstance. Hence when he saw
Our Lord go down to defeat, he sold Him for thirty

pieces of silver. The thief on the left of Our Lord was like Judas. He too, felt the only power worth having was the power of saving him from pain. Hence he cried in agony: "Save thyself and us." In other words, do something external. But the thief on the right moved his pain-racked head toward Our Lord, saw Him divested of every robe of royalty, and denuded of every badge of kingship. And yet he perceived the gold beneath the dust, and the kingdom through a cloud, and power to save a soul beneath the weakness of a drained body: "Lord, remember me when Thou shalt come into Thy Kingdom."

Our Blessed Saviour was so pleased to find His name hallowed amidst blasphemy, and His blessing recognized amidst curses, that He granted the humble prayer of the thief: "Amen, I say to thee, this day thou shalt be with me in Paradise."

The world is full of Judases who think the name of God is hallowed only by worldly pomp and splendor. They forget that the Kingdom of God is internal and "cometh not by observation," and that the Church, which is the Mystical Christ, manifests her greatest strength in the forgiveness of sins.

The world asks: "How can man forgive sin?" It might just as well ask how could a man whose kingdom is no wider than a beam of wood promise the kingdom of heaven to a thief.

The forgiveness of sin is a greater manifestation of the Power of God than the creation of the world. Creation makes something out of nothing. Forgiveness puts something into nothing. But the forgiveness which opens Paradise is obtained as the thief obtained his, namely by asking for it. Pardon, like all gifts of God, is conditioned. The latch on the door of divine forgiveness is on the inside of our soul – on our side, not on God's side. "Behold, I stand at the door and knock." He knocks! He does not force down the door. That would destroy human freedom. He knocks to be admitted; we alone have the power to unlatch the door to invite Him in, that He may sup with us and we with Him. Christ's greatest sorrow is to be denied admittance. "Ye will not come to me." His greatest joy is to be welcomed even by sinners, for "there is more joy in heaven for one sinner doing penance than for ninety-nine just who need not penance." There is no power as strong as the uplifted hand of an absolving priest; there is no joy like the return of a prodigal; there is no peace like the peace of sin forgiven. There is no hope like the hope the thief gives us: Paradise may still be stolen.

The Seven Last Words and the Our Father, 1935

Third Meditation

The Offertory

*"Amen I say to thee, this day thou
shalt be with me in paradise."*

This is now the offertory of the Mass, for our Lord is
offering Himself to His heavenly Father. But in order
to remind us that He is not offered alone, but in union
with us, He unites with His offertory the soul of the
thief at the right. To make His ignominy more
complete, in a master stroke of malice, they crucified
Him between two thieves. He walked among sinners
during His life, so now they let Him hang between
them at death. But He changed the picture, and made
the two thieves the symbols of the sheep and the
goats, which will stand at His right and left hand
when He comes in the clouds of heaven, with His then
triumphant cross, to judge both the living and the
dead.

Both thieves at first reviled and blasphemed, but one
of them, whom tradition calls Dismas, turned his
head to read the meekness and dignity on the face of
the crucified Saviour. As a piece of coal thrown into
the fire is transformed into a bright and glowing
thing, so the black soul of this thief thrown into the

fires of the Crucifixion glowed with love for the Sacred Heart.

While the thief on the left was saying: "If thou be Christ, save thyself and us," the repentant thief rebuked him saying: "Neither dost thou fear God, seeing thou art under the same condemnation. And we indeed justly, for we receive the due reward of our deeds; but this man hath done no evil." That same thief then emitted a plea, not for a place in the seats of the mighty, but only not to be forgotten: "Remember me, when thou shalt come into thy kingdom."

Such sorrow and faith must not go unrewarded. At a moment when the power of Rome could not make Him speak, when His friends thought all was lost and His enemies believed all was won, our Lord broke the silence. He who was the accused, became the Judge: He who was the crucified, became the Divine Assessor of souls, as to the penitent thief He trumpeted the words: "This day thou shalt be with me in paradise." This day -- when you said your first prayer and your last; this day -- thou shalt be with me -- and where I am, there is paradise.

With these words our Lord who was offering Himself to His heavenly Father as the great Host, now unites with Him on the paten of the cross the first small host ever offered in the Mass, the host of the repentant thief, a brand plucked from the burning, a sheaf torn from the earthly reapers; the wheat ground in the mill of the crucifixion and made bread for the Eucharist.

Our Lord does not suffer alone on the Cross; He suffers with us. That is why He united the sacrifice of the thief with His own. It is this St. Paul means when he says that we should fill up those things that are wanting to the sufferings of Christ. This does not mean our Lord on the cross did not suffer all He could. It means rather that the physical, historical Christ suffered all He could in His own human nature, but that the Mystical Christ, which is Christ and us, has not suffered to *our* fullness. All the other good thieves in the history of the world have not yet admitted their wrong and pleaded for remembrances. Our Lord is now in heaven. He therefore can suffer no more in His human nature but He can suffer more in our human natures.

So He reaches out to other human natures, to yours and mine, and asks us to do as the thief did, namely, to incorporate ourselves to Him on the Cross, that sharing in His Crucifixion we might also share in His Resurrection, and that made partakers of His Cross we might also be made partakers of His glory in heaven.

As our Blessed Lord on that day chose the thief as the small host of sacrifice, He chooses us today as the other small hosts united with Him on the paten of the altar. Go back in your mind's eye to a Mass, to any Mass which was celebrated in the first centuries of the Church, before civilization became completely financial and economic. If we went to the Holy Sacrifice in the early Church, we would have brought to the altar each morning some bread and some wine. The priest would have used one piece of that unleavened bread and some of that wine for the sacrifice of the Mass. The rest would have been put aside, blessed, and distributed to the poor. Today we do not bring bread and wine. We bring its equivalent; we bring that which buys bread and wine. Hence the offertory collection.

Why do we bring bread and wine or its equivalent to the Mass? We bring bread and wine because these two things, of all things in nature, most represent the substance of life. Wheat is as the very marrow of the ground, and the grapes its very blood, both of which give us the body and blood of life. In bringing those two things, which give us life, nourish us, *we are equivalently bringing ourselves to* the Sacrifice of the Mass.

We are therefore present at each and every Mass under the appearance of bread and wine, which stand as symbols of our body and blood. We are not passive spectators as we might be watching a spectacle in a theater, but we are co-offering our Mass with Christ. If any picture adequately describes our role in this drama it is this: There is a great cross before us on which is stretched the great Host, Christ. Round about the hill of Calvary are our small crosses on which we, the small hosts, are to be offered. When our Lord goes to His Cross we go to our little crosses, and offer ourselves in union with Him, as a clean oblation to the heavenly Father.

At that moment we literally fulfill to the smallest detail the Saviour's command: Take up your cross daily and follow Me. In doing so, He is not asking us to do anything He has not already done Himself. Nor is it any excuse to say: "I am a poor unworthy host." So was the thief.

Note that there were two attitudes in the soul of that thief, both of which made him acceptable to our Lord. The first was the recognition of the fact that He deserved what He was suffering, but that the sinless Christ did not deserve His Cross; in other words, he was *penitent*. The second was *faith* in Him whom men rejected, but whom the thief recognized as the very King of Kings.

Upon what conditions do we become small hosts in the Mass? How does our sacrifice become one with Christ's and as acceptable as the thief's? Only by reproducing in our souls the two attitudes in the soul of the thief: *penitence and faith*.

First of all we must be penitent with the thief and say: "I deserve punishment for my sins. I stand in need of sacrifice." Some of us do not know how wicked or how ungrateful to God we are. If we did, we would not so complain about the shocks and pains of life. Our consciences are like darkened rooms from which light has been long excluded. We draw the curtain, and lo! everywhere what we thought was cleanliness, we now find dust.

Some consciences have been so filmed over with excuses that they pray with the Pharisee: "I thank Thee, O God, that I am not as the rest of men." Others blaspheme the God of heaven for their pain and sins but repent not. The World War, for example, was meant to be a purgation of evil; it was meant to teach us that we cannot get along without God, but the world refused to learn the lesson. Like the thief on the left, it refuses to be penitent: it refuses to see any relation of justice between sin and sacrifice, between rebellion and a cross.

But the more penitent we are, the less anxious we are to escape our cross. The more we see ourselves as we are, the more we say with the good thief: "I deserved this cross." He did not want to be excused; he did not want to have his sin explained away; he did not want to be let off; he did not ask to be taken down. He wanted only to be forgiven. He was willing even to be a small host on his own little cross -- but that was because he was penitent. Nor is there given to us any other way to become little hosts with Christ in the Mass than by breaking our hearts with sorrow; for unless we admit we are wounded how can we feel the need of healing? Unless we are sorry for our part in the Crucifixion, how could we ever ask to be forgiven its sin?

The second condition of becoming a host in the offertory of the Mass is *faith*. The thief looked above the head of our Blessed Lord and saw a sign which read: "KING." Queer king that! For a crown: thorns. For royal purple: His own blood. For a throne: a cross. For courtiers: executioners. For a coronation: a crucifixion. And yet beneath all that dross the thief saw the gold; amidst all those blasphemies he prayed.

His faith was so strong he was content to remain on his cross. The thief on the left asked to be taken down, but not the thief on the right. Why? Because he knew there were greater evils than crucifixions, and another life beyond the cross. He had faith in the Man on the central cross who could have turned thorns into garlands and nails into rosebuds if He willed; but he had faith in a Kingdom beyond the cross, knowing that the sufferings of this world are not worthy to be compared with the joys that are to come. With the Psalmist his soul cried: "Though I should walk in the midst of the shadow of death I will fear no evils, for thou art with me."

Such faith was like that of the three youths in the fiery furnace who were commanded by the king, Nebuchadnezzar, to adore the golden statue. Their answer was: "For behold our God, whom we worship, is able to save us from the furnace of burning fire, and to deliver us out of thy hands, O king. But if He will not, be it known to thee, O king, that we will not worship thy gods, nor adore the golden statue which thou hast set up." Note that they did not ask God to deliver them from the fiery furnace, though they knew God could do it, "for He is able to save us from the furnace of burning fire." They left themselves wholly in God's hands, and like Job they trusted Him.

So likewise with the good thief: He knew our Lord could deliver Him. But *he did not ask to be taken down from the cross*, for our Lord did not come down Himself even though the mob challenged Him. The thief would be a small host, if need be, unto the very end of the Mass. This did not mean the thief did not love life: He loved life as much as we love it. He wanted life, and a long life, and he found it, for what life is longer than Life Eternal. To each and every one of us in like manner it is given to discover that Eternal Life. But there is no other way to enter it than by penance and by faith which unite us to that Great Host -- the Priest and Victim Christ. Thus do we become spiritual thieves, and steal heaven once again.

Calvary and the Mass, 1936

Fourth Meditation

Blessed Are the Merciful

"Blessed are the merciful: for they shall obtain mercy."

"This day thou shalt be with me in paradise."

At the beginning of His Public Life, on the Hill of the Beatitudes, Our Lord preached: "Blessed are the merciful: for they shall obtain mercy." At the end of His Public Life, on the Hill of Calvary, He practiced that Beatitude as He addressed the thief: "This day you shall be with me in paradise."

The Beatitude of the world is quite different; it runs like this: "Blessed is the man who thinketh first about himself." Life for the world is a struggle for existence in which victory belongs only to the egotists. Liberality, generosity, and graciousness are rare. How often the world insists on "rights," how rarely does it emphasize "duties"; how often it uses the possessive "mine," and how rarely the generous "thine." How full it is of "courts of justice," but how few are its "courts of mercy."

Our Lord came to correct such an exaggerated justice which knew no mercy. Mercy, he reminded us, was something more than a sentimental, emotional tenderheartedness. The very word mercy is derived in Latin from *miserum cor*, a sorrowful heart. Mercy is therefore a compassionate understanding of another's unhappiness.

A person is merciful when he feels the sorrow and misery of another as if it were his own. Disliking misery and unhappiness, the merciful man seeks to dispel the misery of his neighbor just as much as he would if the misery were his own. That is why, whenever mercy is confronted not only with pain, but with sin and wrong-doing, it becomes forgiveness which not merely pardons, but even rebuilds into justice, repentance, and love.

Mercy is one of the dominant notes in the preaching of Our Lord. His parables were parables of mercy. Take for example the hundred sheep, the ten pieces of money, and the two sons. Of the hundred sheep, one was lost; of the ten pieces of money, one was lost; of the two sons, one led a life of dissipation.

It is interesting to note that the lost sheep is the one that was sought, and the shepherd finding it, places it upon his shoulders and brings it into the house rejoicing. But there is no record in the Gospels of any such attention being paid to the ninety-nine sheep who were not lost.

When the woman lost a piece of money and found it, she called in her neighbors to rejoice. But there is no record that she ever called in her neighbors to rejoice in the possession of the other nine which were never lost.

One son went into a foreign country and wasted his substance living riotously. And when he came back, he was given the fatted calf. But the brother who stayed at home was not so rewarded. All these illustrations Our Lord followed with the simple truth: "There shall be more joy in heaven upon one sinner that doth penance than upon ninety-nine just who need not penance."

One day Peter went to Him to inquire just what limitation should be placed upon mercy. And so he asked Our Lord a question about mercy and gave what he thought was rather an extravagant limit: "How often shall my brother offend against me, and I forgive him? till seven times? " And Our Lord answered, "Not till seven times, but till seventy times seven times." And that does not mean four hundred and ninety -- that means infinity.

Developing the idea of infinite mercy, Our Lord said He had come "to heal the contrite of heart"; and that "they that are in health need not a physician, but they that are ill...For I am not come to call the just, but sinners."

Some were scandalized at Him because He "dined with publicans and sinners," but He never ceased to remind us that we should be merciful because the heavenly Father was merciful. "That you may be the children of your Father who is in heaven, who maketh his sun to rise upon the good and bad, and raineth upon the just and the unjust. For if you love them that love you, what reward shall you have? Do not even the publicans do this? ... Be ye therefore perfect as also your heavenly Father is perfect."

Here He is suggesting that we must, like Our Heavenly Father, be merciful to those who according to human estimation least deserve it. That is why he was merciful to Magdalen, to the woman at the well, to Peter who denied him, to Zacchaeus, and even to Judas whom He addressed as "friend."

There was no mistaking His point of view; He was interested in sinners not because of their merits, but because of their misery. And now at the close of His Life, He fulfills the beatitude of mercy in His second word from the Cross.

There were three crosses on Calvary: the crosses of two thieves and the Cross of the Good Shepherd. Of the three who hung silhouetted against that blackened sky, one only was selfish and thought of himself, and that was the thief on the left. He was interested neither in the Saviour who suffered patiently nor in the thief who begged for mercy. He had no thought but for himself as he addressed the Man on the central cross: "If you be Christ, save thyself and us."

The thief on the right, on the contrary, thought not of himself, but about others, namely the thief on the left and Our Blessed Lord. His compassion went out to the thief on the left, because he was not turning to God in this the last hour of his life and begging for forgiveness: "Neither doest thou fear God, seeing thou art under the same condemnation." He also thought of the meek Man crucified between the two of them, who had just prayed for His executioners and was innocent and good: "We indeed (suffer) justly, for we receive the due reward of our deeds; but this man hath done no evil."

It is interesting to inquire why the Merciful Saviour not only forgave the penitent thief, but even gave him the Divine Promise: "This day thou shalt be with me in paradise." Why did not Our Lord address the same words to the thief on the left? The answer is to be found in the Beatitude of Mercy: "Blessed are the merciful: for they shall obtain mercy."

Because the thief on the right was merciful and compassionate, he received mercy and compassion. Because he was thoughtless of self, someone thought of him. There is a law about mercy just as rigid as the laws of nature. What we sow that also we reap. If we sow sparingly we reap sparingly. If we sow generously we reap an abundant harvest. Raised to a spiritual level, this means, as Our Lord has said, "For with what judgment you judge, you shall be judged; and with what measure you mete, it shall be measured to you again."

In other words, by thinking of others we get God to think of us. If the seed of the springtime thought only of self, but never of the soil, the rain, and the sun, it would never bloom and blossom into flower and fruit. But once it forgets itself and goes outside itself, and even dies to seed-life for the sake of the soil and sun and air, lo! it finds itself renewed and beautified a thousand times. If the coal in the bowels of the earth thought only of itself, it would never release its imprisoned sunlight as light and heat.

And so it is with us. Mercy is a compassion which seeks to unburden the sorrows of others as if they were our own. But if we have no such compassion, then how can compassion ever come back to us?

Unless we throw something up, nothing will come down; unless there is an action there can never be a reaction; unless we give, it shall not be given to us; unless we love, we shall not be loved; unless we pardon evil, our evil shall not be forgiven; unless we are merciful to others, God cannot be merciful to us.

If our heart is filled with the sand of our ego, how can God fill it with the fire of his Sacred Heart? If there is no "for sale" sign on the selfishness of our souls, how can God take possession of them?

If then we wish to receive mercy, we must, like the good thief, think of others, for it seems that God finds us best when we are lost in others. *Blessed are the merciful; for they shall obtain mercy.*

In a negative way, Our Lord has reminded us of this Law of Mercy in the parable of the unjust steward: "Therefore is the kingdom of heaven likened to a king, who would take an account of his servants. And when he had begun to take the account, one was brought to him that owed him ten thousand talents. And as he had not wherewith to pay it, his lord commanded that he should be sold, and his wife and children, and all that he had, and payment to be made. But that servant falling down, besought him, saying: "Have patience with me, and I will pay thee all." And the lord of that servant, being moved with pity, let him go and forgave him the debt.

But when that servant was gone out, he found one of his fellow-servants that owed him a hundred pence: and laying hold of him, he throttled him, saying: "Pay what thou owest." And his fellow-servant falling down, besought him, saying: "Have patience with me, and I will pay you all." And he would not, but went and cast him into prison, till he paid the debt.
Now his fellow-servants, seeing what was done, were very much grieved, and they came, and told their lord

all that was done. Then his lord called him and said to him: "Thou wicked servant, I forgave thee all the debt, because thou besoughtest me. Shouldst not thou then have had compassion also on thy fellow-servant, even as I had compassion on thee?" And his lord being angry, delivered him to the torturers until he paid all the debt. So also shall my heavenly Father do to you, if you forgive not everyone his brother from your hearts."

Be merciful then to others, if you would have God kind to you at the last day. Think of others, rather than of yourself. Our Lord has made mercy the very soul of His Church. I think that is the reason why He chose as the head of His Church, not the innocent, not the pure, not the virgin disciple John, but that impetuous, strong man called Peter -- the one who had denied Him, and who, the night of the trial, cursed and swore that he knew not the Man.

His merciful Lord passed him en route to the ignominy of that sorrowful night preceding Good Friday, and Peter, seeing him, went out and "wept bitterly." And tradition adds that Peter wept so much during his life that even his cheeks became furrowed with tears.

And so he who knew by experience the mercy and forgiveness of Our Lord was chosen the head of the Church, in order that the Church might forever practice mercy and kindness.

There is every reason in the world for mercy. There is some good in the worst of us, and there is some bad in the best of us. The good are those who try to find some good in others, and they generally do find it. The evil are those who look for the faults of others, and as a result never see their own.

It was these Our Lord rebuked: "And why seest thou the mote that is in thy brother's eye; and seest not the beam that is in thy own eye? Or how sayest thou to thy brother: Let me cast the mote out of thy eye; and behold a beam is in thy own eye! Thou hypocrite, cast out first the beam of thy own eye, and then shalt thou see to cast out the mote out of thy brother's eye."

If then on the last day we would receive a merciful judgment, we must begin here below to be merciful to others. Just as the clouds release only the moisture which they gathered from the earth, so too can Heaven release only the mercy we have sent heavenward.

By constantly thinking of ourselves, we render ourselves incapable of receiving the kindness of others. Only to the extent that we have emptied ourselves of ourselves can God fill us with Himself. And likewise, the best way to have our prayers answered is to pray for the intentions of others: for God begins to think of us when we cease to think of ourselves.

Therein probably must be sought the reason why more of our prayers are not answered. How can God answer the prayers we address to Him unless we answer the prayers others address to us? Do we answer the prayers of the poor? the maimed? the lame? the sinner? the missionary? If not, then by what right can we expect God to answer our requests?

How can God give us His gifts, if we never give others our gifts? How can God fill our coffers with His treasures, unless we empty them to others?

The law is as simple as that: sow and you reap; do not keep your seed in your barns; give it away -- scatter it over the fields; do the foolish thing; dissipate it, so that even the birds may eat of your bounty. And lo! in a short time you will find your seed increased five, ten, one hundred-fold. But keep it in your barn, and the birds starve and you have no increase.

Give and you shall receive; be merciful and you shall receive mercy. When therefore you are on a cross of pain or sorrow always think of that cross as the cross of the thief on the right.

As such, let your prayers go out to those on the left cross that they may be mindful of the expiatory value of their suffering; let your love also go out to the Good Shepherd on the Central Cross who suffers so innocently for all men, and because you never once thought of yourself but of others, or in other words, because you were merciful, you will hear the reward of Mercy from the Central Cross: "This day you shall be with me in paradise." In that way you become another Good Thief, for a Good Thief is one who steals Paradise!

The Cross and the Beatitudes, 1937

Fifth Meditation

Pain

"This day thou shalt be with me in paradise."

The First Word from the Cross tells us what should be our attitude toward unjust suffering, but the Second Word tells us what should be our attitude toward pain. There are two ways of looking at it; one is to see it without purpose, the other to see it with purpose.

The first view regards pain as opaque, like a stone wall; the other view regards it as transparent, like a window pane. The way we will react to pain depends entirely upon our philosophy of life. As the poet has put it:

> "Two men looked out through their prison bars;
>   The one saw mud, the other stars."

In like manner, there are those who, looking upon a rose, would say: "Isn't it a pity that those roses have thorns"; while others would say: "Isn't it consoling that those thorns have roses!' These two attitudes are manifested in the two thieves crucified on either side of Our Blessed Lord. The thief on the right is the model for those for whom pain has a meaning; the thief on the left is the symbol of unconsecrated suffering.

Consider first the thief on the left. He suffered no more than the thief on the right, but he began and ended his crucifixion with a curse. Never for a moment did he correlate his sufferings with the Man on the central cross. Our Lord's prayer of forgiveness meant no more to that thief than the flight of a bird.

He saw no more purpose in his suffering than a fly sees purpose in the window pane that floods man's habitation with God's warmth and sunlight. Because he could not assimilate his pain and make it turn to the nourishment of his soul, pain turned against him as a foreign substance taken into the stomach turns against it and infects and poisons the whole system.

That is why he became bitter, why his mouth became like a crater of hate, and why he cursed the very Lord Who could have shepherded him into peace and paradise.

The world today is full of those who, like the thief on the left, see no meaning in pain. Knowing nothing of the Redemption of Our Lord they are unable to fit pain into a pattern; it becomes just an odd patch on the crazy quilt of life. Life becomes so wholly unpredictable for them that "a troubled manhood follows their baffled youth."

Never having thought of God as anything more than a name, they are now unable to fit the stark realities of life into His Divine Plan. That is why so many who cease to believe in God become cynics, killing not only themselves but, in a certain sense, even the beauties of flowers and the faces of children for whom they refuse to live.

The lesson of the thief on the left is clear: Pain of itself does not make us better; it is very apt to make us worse. No man was ever better simply because he had an earache. Unspiritualized suffering does not improve man; it degenerates him. The thief at the left is no better for his crucifixion: it sears him, burns him, and tarnishes his soul.

Refusing to think of pain as related to anything else, he ends by thinking only of himself and who would take him down from the cross. So it is with those who have lost their faith in God. To them Our Lord on a cross is only an event in the history of the Roman Empire; He is not a message of hope or a proof of love.

They would not have a tool in their hands five minutes without discovering its purpose, but they live their lives without ever having inquired its meaning. Having no reason for living, suffering embitters them, poisons them, and finally, the great door of life's opportunity is closed in their faces, and like the thief on the left they go out into the night unblessed.

Now look at the thief on the right -- the symbol of those for whom pain has a meaning. At first he did not understand it, and therefore joined in the curses with the thief on the left. But just as sometimes a flash of lightning will illumine the path we have missed, so too the Saviour's forgiveness of His executioners illumined for the thief the road of mercy.

He began to see that if pain had no reason, Jesus would not have embraced it. If the cross had no purpose, Jesus would not have climbed it. Surely He Who claimed to be God would never have taken that badge of shame unless it could be transformed and transmuted to some holy purpose.

Pain was beginning to be comprehensible to the thief; for the present at least it meant an occasion to do penance for his life of crime. And the moment that that light came to him he rebuked the thief on the left saying: "Neither dost thou fear God, seeing thou art under the same condemnation? And we indeed suffer justly, for we receive the due reward of our deeds; but this man hath done no evil" *(Luke 23:40-41).*

Now he saw pain as doing to his soul like to that which fire does to gold: burning away the dross. Or something like that which fever does to disease; killing the germs. Pain was dropping scales away from his eyes; and, turning toward the central cross, he no longer saw a crucified man, but a Heavenly King.

Surely, He Who can pray for pardon for His murderers will not cast off a thief: "Lord, remember me when Thou shalt come into Thy kingdom." Such great faith found its reward: "Amen I say to thee, this day thou shalt be with Me in paradise" *(Luke 23:42-43)*.

Pain in itself is not unbearable; it is the failure to understand its meaning that is unbearable. If that thief did not see purpose in pain he would never have saved his soul. Pain can be the death of our soul, or it can be its life.

It all depends on whether or not we link it up with Him Who, "having joy set before him, endured the cross." One of the greatest tragedies in the world is wasted pain. Pain without relation to the cross is like an unsigned check -- without value. But once we have it countersigned with the Signature of the Saviour on the Cross, it takes on an infinite value.

A feverish brow that never throbs in unison with a Head crowned with thorns, or an aching hand never borne in patience with a Hand on the Cross, is sheer waste. The world is worse for that pain when it might have been so much the better.

All the sick-beds in the world, therefore, are either on the right side of the Cross or on the left; their position is determined by whether, like the thief on the left, they ask to be taken down, or, like the thief on the right, they ask to be taken up.

It is not so much what people suffer that makes the world mysterious; it is rather how much they miss when they suffer. They seem to forget that even as children they made obstacles in their games in order to have something to overcome.

Why, then, when they grow into man's estate, should there not be prizes won by effort and struggle? Cannot the spirit of man rise with adversity as the bird rises against the resistance of the wind? Do not the game fish swim upstream? Must not the alabaster box be broken to fill the house with ointment? Must not the chisel cut away the marble to bring out the form? Must not the seed falling to the ground die before it can spring forth into life? Must not the little streams speed into the ocean to escape their stagnant self-content? Must not grapes be crushed that there may be wine to drink, and wheat ground that there may be bread to eat?

Why then cannot pain be made redemption? Why under the alchemy of Divine Love cannot crosses be turned into crucifixes? Why cannot chastisements be regarded as penances? Why cannot we use a cross to become God-like? We cannot become like Him in His Power: we cannot become like Him in His Knowledge.

There is only one way we can become like Him, and that is in the way He bore His sorrows and His Cross. And that way was with love. "Greater love than this no man hath, that a man lay down his life for his friends." It is love that makes pain bearable.

As long as we feel it is doing good for another, or even for our own soul by increasing the glory of God, it is easier to bear. A mother keeps a vigil at the bedside of her sick child. The world calls it "fatigue" but she calls it love.

A little child was commanded by his mother not to walk the picket fence. He disobeyed and fell, maimed himself and was never able to walk again. Being told of his misfortune he said to his mother: "I know I will never walk again; I know it is my own fault; but if you will go on loving me I can stand anything." So it is with our own pains.

If we can be assured that God still loves and cares, then we shall find joy even in carrying on His redemptive work -- by being redeemers with a small "r" as He is Redeemer with a capital "R." Then will come to us the vision of the difference between Pain and Sacrifice. Pain is sacrifice without love. Sacrifice is pain with love.

When we understand this, then we shall have an answer for those who feel that God should have let us sin without pain:

"The cry of earth's anguish went up unto God, --
'Lord, take away pain, --
The shadow that darkens the world Thou hast made,
The close-coiling chain
That strangles the heart, the burden that weighs
On the wings that would soar, --
Lord, take away pain from the world Thou hast made
That it love Thee the more.'

"Then answered the Lord to the world He had made,
'Shall I take away pain?
And with it the power of the soul to endure
Made strong by the strain?
Shall I take away pity that knits heart to heart
And sacrifice high?
Will ye lose all your heroes who lift from the flame
White brows to the sky?

Shall I take away love that redeems with a price
And smiles through the loss, --
Can ye spare from the lives that would climb unto
mine
The Christ on His Cross?' "

(God and Pain, by George Stewart)

And now this final lesson. You and I often ask God for many favors which are never granted. We can imagine the thief on the right during his life asking God for many favors, and very especially for wealth which was probably not granted. On the other hand, though God does not always grant our material favors, there is one prayer He always grants.

There is a favor that you and I can ask of God this very moment, if we had the courage to do it, and that favor would be granted before the day is over. That prayer which God has never refused and will never refuse is the prayer for suffering. Ask Him to send you a cross and you will receive it!

But why does He not always answer our prayers for *an increase in* salary, for larger commissions, for more money? Why did He not answer the prayer of the thief on the left to be taken down from the cross, and why did He answer the prayer of the thief on the right to forgive his sins?

Because material favors draw us away from Him, but the cross always draws us to Him. And God does not want the world to have us!

He wants us Himself because He died for us!

The Rainbow of Sorrow, 1938

Sixth Meditation

Envy

"This day thou shalt be with me in paradise."

Envy is sadness at another's good, and joy at another's evil. What rust is to iron, what moths are to wool, what termites are to wood, that envy is to the soul: the assassination of brotherly love.

We are not here concerned with just envy or zeal which inspires us to emulate good example and to progress with those who are our betters, for the Scriptures enjoin us to "be zealous for spiritual gifts"; rather, we here touch on that sinful envy which is a wilful grieving at another's good, either spiritual or temporal, for the reason that it seems to diminish our own good. The honor paid to another is regarded by the envious man as a reflected disgrace on himself, and he is sad in consequence. Envy manifests itself in discord, hatred, malicious joy, back-biting, detraction, imputing of evil motives, jealousy, and calumny.

A sample of this kind of envy we find in one of the two women who asked Solomon to adjudicate their dispute. The first woman said, "I and this woman dwelt in one house ... And this woman's child died in the night: for in her sleep, she overlaid him. And rising in the dead time of the night, she took my child from my side while I thy handmaid was asleep ... and laid her dead child in my bosom. "To which the other woman answered: "It is not so as thou sayest, but thy child is dead, and mine is alive."

Since there were no witnesses, Solomon ordered a sword to be brought to him, for he rightly judged that the motherly heart of the real mother would rather give up her child than see it killed. Brandishing the glittering sword, he said, "Divide the living child in two, and give half to the one, and half to the other." Hearing this, the woman whose child was alive cried out in terror and pity, "I beseech thee, my lord, give her the child alive, and do not kill it." But the other said, "Let it be neither mine nor thine, but divide it."

Then the king commanded the child be given to her who would rather give it up to another than have it killed, knowing that she must be the mother. The point of the story is that envy which is so jealous of the good of another may reach a point where it scruples not to take a life.

In our times, envy has taken on an economic form. The avarice of the rich is being matched by the envy of the poor. Some poor hate the rich not because they have unjustly stolen their possessions, but because they want their possessions. Certain *have-nots* are scandalized at the wealth of the *haves*, only because they are tempted by lust for their possessions.

The Communists hate the Capitalists only because they want to be Capitalists themselves; they envy the rich, not because of their need, but because of their greed.

Combined with this is social envy or snobbery which sneers at the higher position of others, because the snobs want to sit in their chairs and enjoy their applause. They assume that in not arriving at such popular favor themselves they were deprived of their due. That is why we hate those who do not pay sufficient attention to us and why we love those who flatter us.

If envy is on the increase today, as it undoubtedly is, it is because of the surrender of the belief of a future life and righteous Divine Justice. If this life is all, they think they should have all. From that point on, envy of others becomes their rule of life.

Our Lord was unceasing in His preaching against envy. To those who were envious of the mercy extended to lost sheep He pictured the angels of Heaven rejoicing more at the one sinner doing penance than at the ninety-nine just who needed not penance. To those who were envious of wealth He warned: "Lay not up to yourselves treasures on earth: where the rust and moth consume, and where thieves break through and steal. But lay up to yourselves treasures in heaven: where neither the rust nor moth consume and where thieves do not break through, nor steal."

To those who were envious of power, such as the Apostles quarreling about first place, He placed a child in the midst of them and, "putting His arms around him" reminded them that heaven was open only to those who were as simple children, for Christ is not in the great but in the little: "Whosoever shall receive one such child as this in my name, receiveth me. And whosoever shall receive me, receiveth not me, but him that sent me."

But His preaching against envy did not save Him from the envious. Pilate was envious of His power; Annas was envious of His innocence; Caiphas was envious of His popularity; Herod was envious of His moral superiority; the Scribes and Pharisees were envious of His wisdom. Each of these had built his judgment seat of mock moral superiority from which to sentence Morality to the Cross. And in order that He might no longer be a person to be envied, they reputed Him with the wicked.

Born between an ox and an ass, they now crucify Him between two criminals. That was the last insult they could give Him. To the public eye they created the impression that three thieves and not two were silhouetted against the sky. In a certain sense, it was true: two stole gold out of avarice; one stole hearts out of love. *Salvandus*, *Salvator* and *Salvatus*: The thief who could have been saved; the thief who was saved; and the Saviour who saved them. The crosses spelled out the words Envy, Mercy, and Pity.

The thief on the left envied the Power which Our Blessed Lord claimed. As the chief priests, scribes, and ancients ridiculed the Saviour, sneering: "He saved others -- himself he cannot save," the thief on the left added to their revilings: "If Thou be Christ, save thyself and us. "In other words: "If I had that power of yours, that power which you claim as the Messiah, I would use it differently than to hang helpless on a tree. I would step down from the Cross, smite my enemies, and prove what power really is."

Thus did Envy reveal that if it had the gifts which it envies in others it would misuse them, as the thief on the left would have surrendered redemption from sin for release from a nail. In like manner many in the world today who are envious of wealth would probably lose their souls if they had that wealth. Envy never thinks of responsibilities. Looking only to self it misuses every gift that comes its way.

Pity has quite a different effect on the soul. The thief on the right had no envy of the Master's Power but only pity for the Master's sufferings. Rebuking his companion on the left, the good thief said: "Neither dost thou fear God, seeing thou art under the same condemnation? And we indeed, justly, for we receive the due reward of our deeds; but this man hath done no evil."

There was not a spark of envy in him. He wanted nothing in all the world, not even to be removed from tragic companioning with his cross. He was not envious of God's Power, for God knows best what to do with His Power. He was not envious of his fellowmen, for they had nothing worth giving.

So he threw himself upon Divine Providence and asked only for forgiveness: "Lord, remember me when thou shalt come into thy kingdom." A dying man asked a dying Man for life; a man without possessions asked a Poor Man for a Kingdom; a thief at the door of death asked to die a thief and steal Paradise. And because He envied nothing, He received all: "Amen, I say to thee, this day thou shalt be with me in Paradise."

One would have thought a saint would have been the first soul purchased over the counter of Calvary by the red coins of redemption, but in the Divine plan, it is a thief who steals that privilege and marches as the escort of the King of Kings into Paradise.

Two lessons are taught us by this Second Word from the Cross. The first is that envy is the source of our wrong judgments about others. The chances are that if we are envious of others, nine times out of ten we will misjudge their characters.

Because the thief on the left was envious of the Power of Our Lord, he misjudged Him and missed both the Divinity of the Saviour and his own salvation. He falsely argued that Power should always be used the way he would have used it, namely to turn nails into rosebuds, a cross into a throne, blood into royal purple, and the blades of grass on the hillside into bayonets of offensive steel.

No one in the history of the world ever came closer to Redemption, and yet no one ever missed it so far. His envy made him ask for the wrong thing; he asked to be taken down when he should have asked to be taken up. It makes one think of how much the envy of Herod resulted in an equally false judgment: He massacred the Innocents because He thought the Infant King came to destroy an earthy kingdom, whereas He came only to announce a heavenly one.

So it is with us. Backbiting, calumny, false judgments, are all born of our envy. We say, "Oh, he is jealous," or "she is jealous"; but how do we know that he or she is jealous unless we ourselves have felt that way? How do we know others are acting proudly unless we know how pride asserts itself? Every envious word is based on a false judgment of our own moral superiority. To sit in judgment makes us feel that we are above those who are judged and more righteous and more innocent than they.

To accuse others is to say: "I am not like that." To be envious of others is to say: "You have stolen that which is mine." Envy of others' wealth has resulted in the gross misjudgment that the best way to do away with its abuse in the hands of the rich is to dispossess them violently, so that the dispossessors may in their turn, enjoy its abuse.

Envy of others' political power has given rise to the erroneous philosophy that even governments may be overthrown if organized violence is strong enough to do so.

Envy thus becomes the denial of all justice and love. In individuals it develops a cynicism that destroys all moral values, for by bankrupting others do we ourselves become bankrupt. In groups it produces a deceit that extends the glad hand of welcome to those who differ, only until they are strong enough to cut it off.

Since envy is so rampant in the world today, it is extremely good counsel to disbelieve 99/100 per cent of the wicked statements we hear about others. Think of how much the thief on the right had to discount to arrive at the truth. He had to disbelieve the judgment of four envious judges, the raillery of envious scribes and ancients, the blasphemous utterances of curious onlookers who loved murders, and the envious taunts of the thief on the left who was willing to lose his soul if only he could keep his fingers nimble for more thefts.

But if he had been envious of the Lord's power, he would never have been saved. He found peace by disbelieving the envious scandalmongers. Our peace is found in the same incredulity.

The chances are that there is a bit of jealousy, a bit of envy, behind every cutting remark and barbed whispering we hear about our neighbor. It is always well to remember that there are always more sticks under the tree that has the most apples. There should be some consolation for those who are so unjustly attacked to remember that it is a physical impossibility for any man to get ahead of us who stays behind to kick us.

A second lesson to be learned from this Word is that the only way to overcome envy is, like the thief on the right, to show pity. As Christians in good faith, we are all members of the Mystical Body of Christ and should therefore love one another as Christ has loved us.

If our arm suffers an injury our whole body feels the pain. In like manner, if the Church in any part of the world suffers martyrdom, we should feel pity toward it as part of our body, and that pity should express itself in prayer and good works. Pity should be extended not only to those outside the Church who are living as if the earth never bore a Cross, but even to the enemies of the Church who would destroy even the shadow of the Cross. God is their Judge; not we.

And as potential brothers of Christ, sons of a Heavenly Father and children of Mary, they must be worth our pity since they were worth the Saviour's Blood. Unfortunately, there are some who blame the Church for receiving great sinners into the Church on their deathbeds.

A few years ago one who was generally believed to be a racketeer and murderer met death at the hands of his fellow criminals. A few minutes before his death, he asked to be received into the Church, was baptized, received First Communion, and was anointed and given the last blessing. Some who should have known better protested against the Church. Imagine! Envy at the salvation of a soul!

Why not rather rejoice in God 's Mercy, for after all did he not belong to the same profession as the thief on the right -- and why should not Our Lord be just as anxious to save twentieth century thieves as first century thieves? They both have souls. It would seem that sinful envy of the salvation of a thief is a greater sin than thievery.

One thief was saved: therefore let no one despair. One thief was lost: therefore let no one presume. Have pity then on the miserable, and Divine Mercy will be the reward for your pity. When the Pharisees accused Our Lord of eating with publicans and sinners He retorted by reiterating the necessity of mercy: "The healthy have no need of a physician, but the sick have. Now go and learn what this means; *I will have mercy and not sacrifice.* For I am not come to call the just, but sinners."

One day a woman went to the saintly Father John Vianney, the Curé of Ars, in France, and said: "My husband has not been to the sacraments or to Mass for years. He has been unfaithful, wicked, and unjust. He has just fallen from a bridge and was drowned -- a double death of body and soul." The Curé answered: "Madam, there is a short distance between the bridge and the water, and it is that distance which forbids you to judge. "

There was just that distance between the two crosses which saved the penitent thief. If the thief on the right had been self-righteous, he would have looked down on Jesus and lost his soul. But because he was conscious of his own sin, he left room for Divine Pardon.

And the answer of the Redeemer to his request proves that to the merciful, love is blind -- for if we love God and our neighbor, who may even be our enemy, Divine Love will go blind as it did for the thief on the right. Christ will no longer be able to see our faults, and that blindness will be for us the dawn of the vision of Love.

THE PENITENT THIEF

"Say, bold but blessed thief,
That in a trice
Slipped into paradise,
And in plain day
Stol'st heaven away,
What trick couldst thou invent
To compass thy intent?
What arms?
What charms?"
"Love and belief."
"Say, bold but blessed thief,
How couldst thou read
A crown upon that head?
What text, what gloss –
A kingdom and a cross?
How couldst thou come to spy
God in a man to die?
What light?
What sight?"
"The sight of grief --"
"I sight to God his pain;
And by that sight
I saw the light,
Thus did my grief
Beget relief.

And take this rule from me,
Pity thou him he'll pity thee.
Use this,
Ne'er miss,
Heaven may be stolen again."

(Anonymous)

Victory Over Vice, 1939

Seventh Meditation

Hope

"This day thou shalt be with me in paradise."

Our concern presently is with two kinds of souls; the despairing and the presumptuous: either those who say, "I am too wicked for God to be interested in me," or those who say, "Oh, I need not worry about my sins. God will take good care of me in the end."

Both these statements are sins of exaggeration. The first is the sin of despair, which exaggerates Divine Justice; the second is the sin of presumption, which exaggerates Divine Mercy. Somewhere there is a golden mean where "Justice and mercy kiss" as the Psalmist puts it, and that is the virtue of Hope.

The *virtue* of Hope is quite different from the *emotion* of Hope. The emotion centers in the body and is a kind of dreamy desire that we can be saved without much effort. The virtue of Hope, however, is centered in the *will* and may be defined as a divinely infused disposition of the will by which with sure confidence, thanks to the powerful help of Almighty God, we expect to pursue eternal happiness, using all the means necessary for attaining it.

The virtue of Hope lies not in the future of time, but beyond the tomb in eternity; its object is not the abundant life of earth, but the eternal love of God.

No stage was ever better set for the drama of Hope than Calvary. Seven centuries before, Isaias had prophesied that Our Divine Lord would be numbered with the wicked. In this hour the prophesy is fulfilled as two thieves, like unholy courtiers, stand unwilling guard on the King of Kings. Nothing could better reveal the contempt in which the Son of God was held than to have crucified Him between two common thieves.

To this ridicule of unholy companionship was added the mockery of a parade that passed before the throne of the central Cross. The Evangelists note them as they pass: *rulers*, soldiers, and passersby. "And the people stood beholding, and the rulers with them derided him, saying: He saved others; let him save himself, if he be Christ, the elect of God" *(Luke 23:35)*. "And the soldiers also mocked him, coming to him, and offering him vinegar" *(Luke 23:36)*. "And they that passed by, blasphemed him, wagging their heads, and saying: Vah, thou that destroyest the temple of God, and in three days dost rebuild it; save thy own self; and if thou be the Son of God, come down from the cross" *(Matthew 27:39-40)*.

As one gazes on that spectacle of three crosses silhouetted against a black and frightened sky, one sees in prospect the future judgment of the world; the Judge in the center and the two divisions of humanity on either side: The sheep and the goats; the blessed and the lost; those who love and those who hate; for the end shall be as the beginning, except that Christ shall appear for the final judgment not on the cross of ignominy but with the cross in glory in the clouds of heaven.

The spiritual development of the thief on the right, reveals how hope is born first out of fear, then out of faith. His conversion began the moment he *feared*. Like the thief on the left he too had blasphemed that Man on the central Cross. Then suddenly turning his head he shouted across the face of Divine Mercy, to his blaspheming fellow thief: "Neither dost thou *fear* God, seeing thou art under the same condemnation? And we indeed justly, for we receive the due reward of our deeds; but this man hath done no evil" *(Luke 23:40-41)*.

The fear of God of which this robber spoke was not a *servile fear* that God would punish them for their thefts; it was rather a *filial fear* based on reverence -- a fear of displeasing Him who had done nothing to deserve such a humiliating death.

There is the first lesson: *Hope begins with fear*; hope involves fear because Hope is not certainty. We can, of course, be certain God will help us and give us sufficient strength to be saved, but we cannot be sure that we will always be faithful to His Grace.

God will not fail us; we need have no fear on that score. But we may fail God. The certitude that I am on the way to God does not exclude the fear that through some fault of mine, I may not come to His Blessed Presence.

Note the next step toward hope in the good thief as his fear led to faith, for "The fear of the Lord . . . is wisdom" *(Job 28:28)*.

In a single moment a soul with a genuine fear of God can come to a greater understanding of the purpose of life than in a lifetime spent in the study of the ephemeral philosophies of men. That is why death-bed conversions may be sincere conversions. The hardened soul disbelieves in God until that awful moment when he has no one to deceive but himself. Once the spark of salutary fear of God had jumped into the soul of the thief from the flaming furnace of that central Cross, fear gave way to faith. His next words were believing.

No longer was Christ an innocent man, nor an exiled upstart, nor a mock monarch. He was a King! Those thorns were His crown; that Cross was His throne; He had Omnipotent Power; that nail was His sceptre; He was a Saviour -- that is why He forgave His enemies.

Out from the full heart of the thief, there welled up the hopeful petition: "Remember me when thou shalt come into thy kingdom" *(Luke 23:42)*. He could not desire what he did not know; he could not hope in what he did not believe. The thief had faith in the Son of God; now he could hope.

And that hope born of fear and faith received its immediate response: "This day thou shalt be with me in paradise" *(Luke 23:43)*.

Above the blasphemous, raucous background of others shouting "Himself He cannot save," he heard: "*This* Day." He had only asked for the future, but the answer was more than he had hoped: "*This* Day." His arms were still pinioned, but he felt them loosen at the sound of "*This* Day"; his body was still racked by pain, but he felt it freshen at *"This* Day." His life was of little value -- but his soul took on eternal worth as he heard "This Day . . . Paradise." A thief had learned to call "Lord" to One whom he despised. And the Lord can forgive sins . . . Such is the beginning of Hope.

Two thieves there were: One who loved and one who hated. Each was on a cross. Neither the good nor the bad ever escape the cross. One thief was saved; therefore, let no one despair. One thief was lost; therefore, let no one presume.

The two extremes to be avoided then are presumption and despair. Presumption is an excess of hope, and despair is a defect of hope. Presumption is an inordinate trust in Divine Mercy, a hope of pardon without repentance, a heaven without merit.

A word to the presumptuous who hope for a death-bed conversion to make their peace with God, and who say: "God would not send me to hell," or "I have lived a fairly decent life, so I have nothing to worry about," or "I know I am a sinner, but no worse than my neighbor; why should I worry? God is merciful."

When you make the statement "God is good," what do you mean? Only this: "God is insensible to evil. He is good because He is unmindful of my wickedness." You forget that God is good *precisely* because He is the enemy of evil. A healthy man is not indifferent to disease; nor is a government good because it ignores crimes and injustice. Why then should you think that God will be complacent about that which you refuse to accept in others?

If you really believed that God is good, would you not be scrupulous about offending Him? Do you not do that much for your friends? The nobler a person is the more you dread offending him. Even for those whom you do not love, you show respect.

Will you then exploit Divine Goodness and deceive One in whom you repose the confidence of salvation? Will you forget that Goodness wounded by cynicism avenges itself?

If you lose your earthly friends by prostituting their generosity, will you not in like manner lose your Heavenly Friend by presuming? Will you make Divine Mercy the excuse for greater sinning? Is there not in every life a *last* pardon as there is also a *last* sin? Have we not allotted to each of us a final sin, which fills up the "bag of sin" and seals our eternity?

You may sin a thousand times and be forgiven, but like the man who threw himself into a river a hundred times, each time to be rescued by the bridge-tender, you may be told by the rescuer: "Someday you will throw yourself into the river and I may not be here to pull you out."

What we all have to realize is that when we sin we turn our back on God. He does not turn His back on us. If we are ever to see His face again we must turn around, that is, turn from sin. That is what is meant by conversion. "Turn ye to me, saith the Lord of hosts" *(Zechariah 1:3).*

God cannot save us without that conversion; if we die in our unrepentant sin we are forever turned away from God. Where the tree falleth there it lies. There is no reversal of values after death.

We cannot love sin during life and begin to love virtue at death. The joys of heaven are the continuance of the Christ-like joys of earth. We do not develop a new set of loves with our last breath. We shall reap in eternity only what we sowed on earth. If we loved sin, we shall reap corruption; but we shall never gather grapes from thistles.

The Justice of God is not separable from His Goodness. If He were not Just, He would not be Good. Because He is Goodness, His Justice pardons; because He is Justice, His Goodness expiates. The thief on the right saw the need of Justice the moment he admitted, "We suffer justly"; that is why immediately he felt the response of Goodness: "This Day . . . Paradise."

Then let not our presuming moderns who pile sin on sin think that they can insult God until their lease on life has run out and then expect an eternal lease on one of the Father's mansions. Did He who went to Heaven by a Cross intend that you should go there by sinning?

Let us consider the other type of soul: the despairing. As presumption forgets Divine Justice, so despair forgets Divine Mercy. Modern despair is not only hopeless about eternal life, which it doubts, but even about earthly life, which it mocks. Never before in the history of Christianity has despair been so abysmal. Today there is everywhere an anticipation of catastrophe, an appalling sense of unpredictability and impending disaster.

In the past, men recovered from despair either by returning to the glories of the past or by looking forward to a crown beyond the cross; but now that minds have lost faith in God, they have only this world to give them hope.

Since that has turned against them they feel a conscious rupture with hope. They curse a meaningless existence, succumb to a continuous exasperation with uncertainty, and yield to a suicidal intent to escape the inescapable.

There are two causes for modern despair: Sensuality and sadness. It is a fact that those poets who have most ridiculed the future life and those writers who have poured the most scorn on sin and Divine Justice were themselves most abandoned to sensuality.

The singers of voluptuousness are always the singers of despair. This is because sensuality produces continuous disillusionment. Its pleasures must be repeated because of their *unsatisfyingness*; therefore, they make hungry where most they satisfy.

Being deceived so many times by the alluring promises of the flesh, its addicts feel that all life is a deceit. Having been fooled by that which promised pleasure, they conclude that nothing can give pleasure. The fruit of pessimism blossom on the tree of a dissolute life.

From another point of view sensuality begets despair because by its very nature it is directed to a sensual object, and an excessive dedication to the carnal kills the capacity for the spiritual. Delicate hands lose their skill by handling rough stones, and souls lose their appetite for the Divine by undue attachment to the flesh. The eyes that refuse to look upon the light soon lose their power to see: "Having eyes, [they] see . . . not" *(Mark 8:18)*.

Hope implies love; but if love is centered in the corporal, the soul is deadened to all that is not carnal: It finds less and less satisfaction in duty, family, work, profession, and, above all else, God. There is time only for the wicked joy to which one is slave.

Naturally, the future life and heaven and the Cross cease to move such a person. There is no desire except the biological; the future begins to be disgusting. From a stage where there is no time for God, they reach another where there is no taste for God. Thus does a world, which forgot love for sex, pay its terrible penalty in the despair, which calls life meaningless because it has made its own life a wreck.

The second cause of despair is sadness. Sadness does not mean sorrow caused by a death, but rather a surrender to states of depression because of a consciousness of sin and unworthiness. Many falls produce melancholy; repeated defeats induce despair.

St. Paul speaks of carnal excesses and greed for money as the feeble compensations for the one who experiences melancholy induced by multiplied sin: "Who despairing have given themselves up to lasciviousness, unto the working of all uncleanness unto covetousness" *(Ephesians 4:19)*.

Despair, born of the loss of God, also ends in persecution. In their impiety, such souls would kill the God they left. That is why wherever you find an atheistic government in the world today, you find "purges." Not being able to tolerate their own inner sadness, they must compensate for it by killing hope in others.

Each despairing soul must decide for itself the reason for despair. Regardless however of how multiplied or grievous your sins may have been, there is still room for hope. Did not Our Lord say: "For I came not to call the just, but sinners" *(Mark 2:17)*; and on another occasion "there shall be joy in heaven upon one sinner that doth penance, more than upon ninety-nine just who need not penance" *(Luke 15:7)*.

If He forgave the thief, and Magdalene, and Peter, why not you? What makes many in old age sad is not that their joys are gone, but that their hopes are gone. Your earthly hopes may decrease with the years, but not heavenly hope. Regardless of the sinful burden of the years, God's mercy is greater than your faults.

Only when God ceases to be infinitely merciful and only when you begin to be infinitely evil, will there be reason for despair; and that will be *never*; Peter denied Our Lord, but Our Lord did not deny Peter. The thief cursed Christ, but He did not curse the thief. If we had never sinned, we could never call Christ Saviour.

The Divine Invitation has never been annulled: "Come to me, all you that labour, and are burdened, and I will refresh you" *(Matthew 11:28)*. That invitation is not only for the weary, it is also for the sinful.

If you insist that you are disgusted with yourself, remember that you can come to God even by a succession of disgusts. What does your disgust mean except that everything earthly has failed you? That is one of the ways God makes you feel hunger for the Divine. Do you not crave food most when you are hungry? Do you not want water most when you are thirsty?

Your own disgust, if you knew it, is the distant call of Divine Mercy. If then the poverty of your merits makes you shrink from the Divine Presence, then let your needs draw you to Him.

The principal reason for the increase of nervous disorders in the world is due to *hidden guilt* or unatoned sin locked on the inside until it festered.

These souls are running off to psychoanalysts to have their sins explained away, when what they need is to get down on their knees and right themselves with God.

When disgusted with our sins we can go into a confessional box, become our own accuser, hear the words of absolution Our Lord Himself gave, make amends and start life all over again, for none of us want our sins explained away; we want them forgiven. That is the miracle of the Sacrament of Penance and the rekindling of Hope.

"If I had sat at supper with the Lord
And laid my head upon that saving breast
I might have turned and fled among the rest –
I might have been that one who left the board
To add the high priests' silver to his hoard.
Had our Redeemer stooped to wash my feet,
Would I have washed my neighbor's clean and sweet
Or thrice denied the Christ I had adored?

"Long have I grieved that I was not St. Paul
Who rode those seas and saw the tempest toss
The ships he sailed in when he heard the call
To preach the risen Christ and gain through loss.
Tonight I envy most among them all
That thief who hung repentant on his cross."
                                    (Alexander Harvey)

The Seven Virtues, 1940

Eighth Meditation

A Word to the Sinners

There are two ways of coming to God: through the preservation of innocence; and through the loss of it. Some have come to God because they were good, like Mary, who was "full of grace"; like Joseph, the "just man"; like Nathaniel, "in whom there was no guile"; or like John the Baptist, "the greatest man ever born of woman."

But others have come to God who were bad like the young man of the Gerasenes "possessed of devils," like Magdalen, out of whose corrupt soul the Lord cast seven devils; and like the thief at the right who spoke the second word to the Cross.

The world loves the mediocre. The world hates the very good and the very bad. The good are a reproach to the mediocre, and the evil are a disturbance. That is why Christ was crucified with thieves. Seven hundred years before, Isaiah had prophesied that He would be "reputed with the wicked" *(Isaiah 53:12)*. Luke verified it: "And with the wicked was he reckoned" *(Luke 22: 37)*.

So it was willed by God. This is His true position: Jesus among the worthless ones. During his life He was accused of eating and drinking with sinners; now they can accuse Him of dying with them. And these companions on their crosses were not political prisoners, nor castoff capitalists from a proletarian revolution; they were just plain bandits -- pure and simple.

Here is a supreme instance of the Right Man in the right place: Christ among the bandits; the Redeemer in the midst of the unredeemed; the Physician among the lepers -- for God does not work through culture but through grace. He does not ask men to be refined; He asks them to be penitent. Thus does God show that we become great not because of what we are, but because of what He gives.

God in His Infinite Wisdom had reached deep into the lower layers of humanity and picked out of its dregs two worthless derelicts; and He used one of them as the escort of His Eternal Son.

At the beginning of the Crucifixion they both cursed and blasphemed the Saviour. But suddenly the soul of one, lighted by fires from that Central Cross, turned to a King who was being mocked and asked to be one of His subjects: "Lord, remember me when thou shalt come into thy kingdom" *(Luke 23:42).*

Lord: He called Him Lord! A real King is so easy to approach!

Remember me: There was a touch of humor in asking God to remember. God had remembered him before he was born. That is why He is immortal. God had been following his soul down the corridors of time, and now the pursued asks the Pursuer to remember.

When thou shalt come into thy kingdom: How did the thief know He had a Kingdom? Maybe the crown of thorns spoke of a diadem, the crucifixion of a coronation, the nails of a sceptre, and the blood of royal purple. We can never judge people by the way they are dressed!

No prayer to God is ever unanswered. From the Central Cross there flashed back: "This day thou shalt be with me in Paradise" *(Luke 23:43)*.

This day: Evil has its hour, but God has His day.

Thou: "And he calleth his own sheep by name *(John 10:3)*. This was the foundation of Christian Democracy. The soul of an outcast is of such value that the Eternal Word addresses him in the second person singular: "Thou."

Shalt be with me in Paradise: I wonder why He said in Paradise? To be with Him is Paradise.

The mob on Calvary asked Him to come down from the Cross: the thief asked to be taken up! The masses would have believed if He preached a religion without a Cross; the thief found his faith by hanging on a cross. This is the supreme instance of one bringing good out of evil. It is doubtful if the thief would have found Goodness otherwise!

Why is it that this thief found salvation? Why, on the other hand, did Our Lord say to the chief priests and the ancients: "Amen I say to you, that the publicans and the harlots shall go into the kingdom of God before you" *(Matthew 21:3)*? Why did He lash out with whips at the merchants, and with His tongue scourge the so-called good people, calling them a "brood of vipers" and "whitened sepulchres"? And while speaking harshly to this group, why did he speak so kindly to the woman with five husbands, so gently to the publican Matthew, and so courteously to the good thief?

It can only be because the capacity for conversion is greater in the really wicked than in the self-satisfied and complacent. The very emptiness of soul of the sinners is in itself an occasion for receiving the compassion of God. Self-disgust is the beginning of conversion, for it marks the death of pride.

The prodigal began to be converted only when he was hungry: "There was a famine." He had left the Father's House saying: "Give me," but he came back

saying: "Father, *make me* one of thy hired servants."
As the Mother of Our Lord had said of her Son: "He
hath filled the hungry with good things; and the rich
he hath sent empty away" *(Luke 1:53).*

May it not be that the conversion of the good thief is
the key to the conversion of the modem world? Men
will return to God, not because they are good, but
because they recognize that they are evil. They will
come to God through evil rather than through
goodness. Or shall we say they will come to God
through the Devil.

Countless are the instances mentioned in the Gospel
of those who came to God after Satan was driven from
their souls. The French Revolutionist Sorel predicted
that the basic problem of the twentieth century
would be the problem of evil.

The 19th century foreshadowed this in two of its
most outstanding writers: Dostoevski, the Russian,
and Nietzsche, the German. Nietzsche, representing
one side of the problem of evil, believed that the
world must pass from Christ to anti-Christ;
Dostoevski, representing the other side, believed that
the world would be saved by passing from anti-Christ
to Christ.

Most typical of the latter approach is Professor C.E.M.
Joad of the University of London, who explains the
fanaticism for such creeds of Nazism, Fascism, and

Communism as the yearning of irreligious minds to fill up the moral vacuum in their souls by an object of absolute adoration -- an evil god.

The universality of evil throughout the world frightened Joad, and "so pervasive and insistent have these evils become that it is at times difficult to avoid concluding that the Devil has been given a longer rope than usual for the tempting and corrupting of men."

None of the explanations given by his contemporaries concerning evil are satisfactory. The socialist explanation of evil in terms of economic inequality and injustice, Joad rejects; for if poverty is the root of all evil, then money must be the source of all virtue.

The psychological explanation of evil attributes evil to suppressed desires, thwarted sex libidos, and mother libidos, all of which could be abolished by popularizing aesthetics, by extending the blessings of the machine and the ballot.

These he rejected after asking himself: "Was no rich man ever cruel, was no unrepressed man ever tyrannical," "was no self-expressive child selfish"?

With the posing of the question, there begins to file before the mind's eye that long line of absolute rulers, the sultans, the caliphs, the emperors and the kings, with the smaller fry, the school masters and the work house superintendents, and the slave overseers, the Squeerses and Brooklehursts, and Bumbles and Murdestones, bringing up the rear of the melancholy procession, who had money enough to be exempt from the cramping effects of poverty and power enough to be free from the repressive effects of authority.

Yet they used their power to increase, and often deliberately to increase, the misery of human beings with such consistency as to provoke Lord Acton's terrible verdict: "All Power corrupts and absolute power corrupts absolutely."

None of the modem explanations of evil, Joad argues, explains the fact of evil. "Evil is not merely a by-product of unfavorable circumstances; it is too wide-spread and too deep-seated to admit of any such explanations; so wide-spread, so deep-seated that one can only conclude that what the religions have taught is true, and that evil is *endemic in the heart of man.*"

"Endemic in the heart of man!" That is it. It is in our blood! It flows through our veins! It gives life to the brain when it thinks evil; it energizes the will when it kills; it fires the muscle when it drops bombs; and it persecutes the prayerful.

In the face of that evil which is endemic in the human heart, this truth emerges: It is one thing to be blind and another thing to know it.

There is hope for those who are deaf and who want to hear and for the lame who want to walk, and there is hope for the diseased who acknowledges the need of a physician and the sinner who feels the need of a redeemer.

The thief at the right conquered evil that way: By admitting his emptiness of soul he called upon God to save him! There is only one thing in the world worse than sin, and that is denying that we are sinners.

The tragedy of the modern world is that so many deny sin. Never before in the history of the world was there so much evil, and never before was there so little consciousness of it. Talk to a modern man about reconciling his soul with God and he will say: "What have I ever done to Him? I let Him alone, why should He not leave me alone?"

Why does he say this? For the same reason a healthy man would say to a surgeon who wanted to operate on him: "There is nothing wrong with me. Leave me alone." In like manner if you are your own law, if you set your own standards, and if you are your own god, then it is nonsense to ask to be reconciled to another god.

As a man gets more wicked he understands his wickedness less and less, just as when a man's fever climbs to a point of deliriousness, he understands his sickness less and less. He may even think himself so healthy that he wants to go to work. A moderately bad man always thinks he is good. We never know we were asleep until we wake up, and we never know what sin really is until we get out of it.

Only when you are sick, do you ask for a physician; and only when you recognize yourself as a sinner, do you ask for your Redeemer. Our Lord said: "They that are in health need not a physician, but they that are ill" *(Matthew 9:12)*.

When, therefore, you reach a point where you cease calling yourself "idiotic" (and don't mean it) -- and begin to call yourself a "rotter" (and mean it) -- you are on the pathway of the good bandit that leads to conversion. The perception of guilt is the condition of conversion, as the perception of disease is the condition of remedy. So long as we think we are good we will never find God.

If therefore we think that we know it all, how can God teach us what we do not know?

We admit sometimes that we are ill tempered, or that we are intemperate, but will we ever admit that we are proud? We condemn pride so vociferously in others, but we deny that we have ever been guilty.

The more conceited we are, the more we hate conceit in others. The more we say, "I am not conceited," the more we prove that we are conceited.

Our pride makes us look down on people, so that we can never look up to God. In fact because our pride admits no law and no authority other than ourselves, it is essentially anti-God.

All our other sins can be from ourselves; for example, avarice, lust, anger and gluttony. But pride comes direct from hell. By that sin fell the angels. It destroys the very possibility of conversion.

If therefore we can humble ourselves as did the thief at the right, and admit we have done wrong, then out of our creative despair we can cry to the Lord to remember us in our misery! The very moment we stop shutting and posing and begin to see ourselves as we really are, then in our humility we shall be exalted.

Let us examine our consciences. Let us ask ourselves not how *much* we know, but how much we do not know; not how good we are, but how bad we are. Let us judge ourselves not by the knowledge we possess, but by our consciences; not by our education, but by our habits; not by our politeness, but by our hearts.

As soon as we feel a great void in our souls, and realize that by our sinning we are no longer our own, and acknowledge that we are still thirsty at the border of a well, and admit that we have played the fool, and that our follies of the years mount up in their dark arrears, then out of a dark and swampy soul, we cry out with the thief -- as all Catholics do when we go to Confession -- "Bless me Father, for I have sinned" -- "I am a sinner."

Such is the beginning of salvation. The thief died a thief, for he stole Paradise. And if we win Paradise we will be thieves too, for we will never deserve what we got -- the God of everlasting peace!

Seven Words to the Cross, 1944

Ninth Meditation

The Secret of Sanctity

There is only one thing in the world that is definitely and absolutely your own, and that is your will. Health, power, possessions, and honor can all be snatched from you, but your will is irrevocably your own, even in hell. Hence, nothing really matters in life, except what you do with your will. It is that which makes the story of the two thieves crucified on either side of Our Lord, for here is the drama of wills.

Both thieves at first blasphemed. There was no such thing as the good thief at the beginning of the Crucifixion. But when the thief on the right heard that Man on the Central Cross forgive His executioners, he had a change of soul.

He began to accept his sorrows. He took up his cross as a yoke rather than as a gibbet, abandoned himself to God's Will, and turning to the rebellious thief on the left said: "Neither dost thou fear God, seeing thou art under the same condemnation? And we indeed justly: for we receive the due reward of our deeds. But this man hath done no evil" *(Luke 23:40-41).*

Then from his heart already so full of surrender to His Saviour, there came this plea, "Remember me when thou shalt come into thy kingdom" *(Luke 23:42)*. Immediately there came the answer: "Amen I say to thee: this day thou shalt be with me in paradise" *(Luke 23:43)*.

"Thou." We are all individuals in the sight of God. He called His sheep by name. This word was the foundation of Christian democracy. Every soul is precious in God's sight, even those whom the state casts out and kills.

At the foot of the cross, Mary witnessed the conversion of the good thief, and her soul rejoiced that he had accepted the Will of God. Her Divine Son's second word promising Paradise as a reward for that surrender, re-minded her of her own Second Word thirty years before, when the angel had appeared to her and told her that she was to be the Mother of Him Who was now dying on the Cross.

In her First Word, she asked how this would be accomplished since she knew not man. But when the angel said she would conceive of the Holy Spirit, Mary immediately answered: "Be it done to me according to thy word" *Fiat mihi* secundum verbum tuum. *(Luke 1:38)*

This was one of the great Fiats of the world. The first was at Creation when God said: *Fiat Lux*: "Let there be light"; another was in Gethsemani, when the Saviour, pressing the chalice of redemption to his lips, cried: *Fiat voluntas tua*: "Thy will be done" *(Matthew 26:42)*. The third was Mary's, pronounced in a Nazarene cottage, which proved to be a declaration of war against the empire of evil; *Fiat mihi* secundum verbum tuum: "Be it done to me according to thy word" *(Luke 1:38)*.

The Second Word of Jesus on Golgotha and the second Word of Mary in Nazareth teach the same lesson: *Everyone in the world has a cross, but the cross is not the same for any two of us.* The cross of the thief was not the cross of Mary. The difference was due to God's will toward each. The thief was to give life; Mary to accept life. The thief was to hang on his cross; Mary was to stand beneath hers. The thief was to go ahead; Mary to remain behind. The thief received a dismissal; Mary received a mission. The thief was to be received into Paradise, but Paradise was to be received into Mary.

Each of us, too, has a cross. Our Lord said: "If any man will follow me" *(Mark 8:34)*. He did not say: "Take up my cross." My cross is not the same as yours, and yours is not the same as mine. Every cross in the world is tailor made, custom built, patterned to fit one and no one else.

That is why we say: "My cross is hard." We assume that other persons' crosses are lighter, forgetful that the only reason our cross is hard is simply because it is our own. Our Lord did not make His Cross; it was made for Him. So yours is made by the circumstances of your life, and by your routine duties. That is why it fits so tightly. Crosses are not made by machines.

Our Lord deals separately with each soul. The crown of gold we want may have underneath it the crown of thorns, but the heroes who choose the crown of thorns often find that underneath it is the crown of gold. Even those that seem to be without a cross actually have one.

No one would have ever suspected that when Mary resigned herself to God's Will by accepting the honor of becoming the Mother of God, she would ever have to bear a cross. It would seem, too, that one who was preserved free from original sin should be dispensed from the penalties of that sin, such as pain. Yet this honor brought to her seven crosses and ended by making her the Queen of Martyrs.

There are, therefore, as many kinds of crosses as there are persons: crosses of grief and sorrow, crosses of want, crosses of abuse, crosses of wounded love and crosses of defeat.

There is the cross of widows. How often Our Lord spoke of them, for example, in the parable of the judge and the widow *(Luke 18:1-8)*; when He rebuked the Pharisees who "devour the houses of widows" *(Mark 12:40)*, when he spoke to the widow of Naim *(Luke 7:12)*, and when He praised the widow who threw two mites into the temple treasury *(Mark 12:42)*. Widowhood may have been particularly dear to Him, because His own mother was a widow, for Joseph His foster-father was presumably already dead.

When God takes someone from us, it is always for a good reason. When the sheep have grazed and thinned the grass in the lower regions, the shepherd will take a little lamb in his arms, carry it up the mountain where the grass is green, lay it down, and soon the other sheep will follow. Every now and then Our Lord takes a lamb from the parched field of a family up to those Heavenly Green pastures, so that the rest of the family may keep their eyes on their true home and follow through.

Then there is the cross of sickness, which always has a Divine purpose. Our Blessed Lord said: "This sickness is not unto death, but for the glory of God: that the Son of God may be glorified by it" *(John 11:4)*. Resignation to this particular kind of cross is one of the very highest forms of prayer. Unfortunately, the sick generally want to be doing something else other than the thing that God wants them to do.

The tragedy of this world is not so much the pain in it; the tragedy is that so much of it is wasted. It is only when a log is thrown into the fire that it begins to sing. It was only when the thief was thrown into the fire of a cross that he began to find God. It is only in pain that some begin to discover where Love is.

Because our crosses differ, soul will differ from soul in glory. We think too often that in Heaven there is going to be somewhat the same equality in social positions that we have here; that servants on earth will be servants in heaven; that the important people on earth will be the important people in heaven. This is not true.

God will take into account our crosses. He seemed to suggest that in the parable of Dives and Lazarus: "Son, remember that thou didst receive good things in thy lifetime, and likewise Lazarus evil things: but now he is comforted and thou art tormented" *(Luke 16:25)*.

There will be a bright jewel of merit for those who suffer in this world. Because we live in a world where position is determined economically, we forget that in God's world the royalty are those who do His Will. Heaven will be a complete reversal of values of earth. The first shall be last and the last first, for God is no respecter of persons.

A wealthy and socially important woman went to heaven. St. Peter pointed to a beautiful mansion and said: "This is your chauffeur's home." "Well," said she, "if that is his home, think what mine will be like." Pointing to a tiny cottage, Peter said: "There is yours." "I can't live in that," she answered. And Peter said: "I'm sorry, that is the best I could do with the material you sent me." Those who suffer as the thief did have sent ahead some fine material.

It makes no difference what you do here on earth; what matters is the love with which you do it. The street cleaner who accepts in God's name a cross arising from his state in life, such as the scorn of his fellowmen; the mother who pronounces her *Fiat* to the Divine Will as she raises a family for the Kingdom of God; the afflicted in hospitals who say *Fiat* to their cross of suffering are the uncanonized saints, for what is sanctity but fixation in goodness by abandonment to God's Holy Will?

It is typically American to feel that we are not doing anything unless we are doing something *big*. But from the Christian point of view, there is no one thing that is bigger than any other thing. The bigness comes from the way our wills utilize things. Hence mopping an office for the love of God is bigger than running the office for the love of money.

Most of our misery and unhappiness come from rebellion against our present state coupled with false ambition. We become critical of everyone above us, as if the cloak of honor, which another wears, was stolen from our shoulders. Rest assured that if it is God's Will that we do a certain task, it will be done, though the whole world would rise up and say "Nay." But if we get that honor by the abandonment of truth and humility, it will be bitter as wormwood and as biting as gall.

Each of us is to praise and love God in his own way. The bird praises God by singing, the flower by blooming, the clouds with their rain, the sun with its light, the moon with its reflection, and each of us by the patient resignation to the trials of his state in life.

In what does your life consist except two things? 1) Active duties. 2) Passive circumstances. The first is under your control; these do in God's name. The second is outside your control; these submit to in God's name. Consider only the present; leave the past to God's Justice the future to His Providence. Perfection of personality does not consist in knowing God's plan, but in submitting to it as it reveals itself in the circumstances of life.

There is really one shortcut to sanctity; the one Mary chose in the Visitation, the one Our Lord chose in Gethsemani, the one the thief chose on the Cross -- abandonment to the Divine Will.

If the gold in the bowels of the earth did not say *Fiat* to the miner and the goldsmith, it would never become the chalice of the altar. If the pencil did not say *Fiat* to the hand of the writer, we would never have the poem; if Our Lady did not say *Fiat* to the angel, she would never have become the House of Gold; if Our Lord did not say *Fiat* to the Father's Will in Gethsemani, we would never have been redeemed; if the thief did not say *Fiat* in his heart, he never would have been the escort for the Master into Paradise.

The reason most of us are what we are, mediocre Christians, "up" one day, "down" the next, is simply because we refuse to let God work on us. As crude marble, we rebel against the hand of the sculptor; as unvarnished canvas we shrink from the oils and tints of the Heavenly Artist. We are so "fearful lest having Him we may have nought else beside," forgetful that if we have the fire of Love, why worry about the sparks, and if we have the perfect round, why trouble ourselves with the arc.

We always make the fatal mistake of thinking that it is what we do that matters, when really what matters is what we let God do to us. God sent the angel to Mary, not to ask her to do something, but to let something be done.

Since God is a better artisan than you, the more you abandon yourself to Him, the happier He can make you. It is well to be a self-made man, but it is better to be a God-made man.

God will love you, of course, even though you do not love Him, but remember if you give Him only half your heart, He can make you only fifty percent happy. You have freedom only to give it away. To whom do you give yours? You give it either to the moods of the hour, to your egotism, to creatures or to God.

Do you know that if you give your freedom to God, in heaven you will have no freedom of choice, because once you possess the Perfect, there is nothing left to choose. And still you will be perfectly free, because you will be One with Him Whose Heart is Freedom and Love!

Seven Words of Jesus and Mary, 1945

Acknowledgments

To the Archbishop Fulton John Sheen Foundation in Peoria, Illinois for their help and encouragement in the creation of this book series on the Seven Last Words.

We would also like to acknowledge the Most Rev. Daniel R. Jenky, C.S.C., Bishop of Peoria, in appreciation for his many years of leadership and fidelity to Archbishop Sheen's cause for canonization.

www.archbishopsheencause.org

To the staff at Sophia Institute Press, for their invaluable assistance on this project and their mission to nurture the spiritual, moral and cultural life of souls and to spread the gospel of Christ in conformity with the authentic teachings of the Roman Catholic Church is very much appreciated.

www.sophiainstitute.com

We value the guidance, support, and prayers of the good folks at Bishop Sheen Today for helping us to share the wisdom of Archbishop Fulton J. Sheen with a whole new generation of readers. Your apostolic work of sharing his audio and video presentations along with his many writings to a worldwide audience is very much appreciated.

www.bishopsheentoday.com

And lastly, to Archbishop Fulton J. Sheen, whose teachings on the Holy Hour and prayer continue to inspire many to love God more and to appreciate the gift of the Church. May we be so blessed as to imitate Archbishop Sheen's love for the saints, the sacraments, the Eucharist, and the Blessed Virgin Mary. May the Good Lord grant him a very high place in heaven!

About The Author

Fulton J. Sheen
(1895–1979)

Archbishop Sheen, best known for his popularly televised and syndicated television program, Life is Worth Living, is held today as one of Catholicism's most widely recognized figures of the twentieth century.

Fulton John Sheen, born May 8, 1895 in El Paso, Illinois was raised and educated in the Roman Catholic faith. Originally named Peter John Sheen, he came to be known as a young boy by his mother's maiden name, Fulton. Over the course of many dedicated, steadfast years, he was ordained a priest of the Diocese of Peoria at St. Mary's Cathedral in Peoria, IL on September 20, 1919.

Following his ordination, Sheen moved overseas to further his education, and earned a doctorate in Philosophy from The Catholic University of Louvain in Belgium in 1923. That same year, he received the Cardinal Mercier Prize for International Philosophy, becoming the first ever American to earn this distinction.

Upon returning to America after varied and extensive work throughout Europe, Sheen continued to preach, as well as teach theology and philosophy at the Catholic University of America in Washington D.C. from 1927 until 1950.

Starting in 1930, Sheen became a host on a weekly Sunday night radio broadcast called The Catholic Hour. This broadcast captured many devoted listeners, reportedly drawing an audience of four million people every week for two decades.

In 1950, he became the National Director of the Society for the Propagation of the Faith, raising money to support the missions. During the 16 years that he held this position, he raised millions of dollars to support the missionary activity of the Church. These efforts influenced tens of millions of people all over the world, bringing them to know Christ and his Church. In addition, his own preaching and personal example brought about many converts to Catholicism.

In 1951, Sheen was appointed Auxiliary Bishop of the Archdiocese of New York. That same year, Sheen moved from his weekly radio broadcast to hosting the Catholic television program, Life is Worth Living. This show aired every Tuesday evening at 8pm for six years.

Over the course of the show, Sheen's Life is Worth Living competed for airtime with popular television stars such as Frank Sinatra and Milton Berle. Sheen's show held its own, and in 1953, just two years after its debut, he won an Emmy Award for "Most Outstanding Television Personality." Fulton Sheen credited the Gospel writers - Matthew, Mark, Luke, and John - for their valuable contribution to his success. This television show ran until 1957, boasting as many as 30 million weekly viewers.

In the fall of 1966, Sheen was appointed Bishop of Rochester, New York. During this time, Bishop Sheen hosted another television series, The Fulton Sheen Program; running from 1961 to 1968 that closely modeled the Life is Worth Living series.

After nearly three years as Bishop of Rochester, Fulton Sheen resigned and was appointed the Archbishop of Titular See of Newport Wales by Pope Paul VI. This new appointment allowed Sheen the flexibility to continue preaching.

Sheen was known for his annual Good Friday homilies that he preached for 58 consecutive years in New York and elsewhere. Sheen also led numerous retreats for priests and religious, and preached at conferences all over the world.

When asked by Pope Pius XII how many converts he had made, Sheen responded, "Your Holiness, I have never counted them. I am always afraid if I did count them, I might think I made them, instead of the Lord."

"If you want people to stay as they are," he said, "tell them what they want to hear. If you want to improve them, tell them what they should know." This he did, not only in his preaching but also in the numerous books and articles he wrote. His book entitled 'Peace of Soul' was sixth on the New York Times best-seller list.

Three of Sheen's great loves were for the Missions and the propagation of the faith; the Blessed Mother; and the Eucharist.

He made a daily holy hour before the Blessed Sacrament, from which he drew strength and inspiration to preach the gospel and in the presence of which he prepared his homilies. "I beg [Christ] every day to keep me strong physically and alert mentally in order to preach His gospel and proclaim His Cross and Resurrection," he said. "I am so happy doing this that I sometimes feel that when I come to the good Lord in Heaven, I will take a few days' rest and then ask Him to allow me to come back again to this earth to do some more work."

His contributions to the Catholic Church are numerous and varied, ranging from educating in classrooms, churches, and homes, to preaching over a nationally publicized radio show, and two television programs, as well as penning over 50 written works. Bishop Fulton J. Sheen had a gift for communicating the Word of God in the most pure, simple way. His strong background in philosophy helped him to relate to all of his followers in a highly personalized manner. His timeless messages continue to have great relevance today. He inspires each of us to live a God-centered life with the joy and love that God intended.

On October 2, 1979 Archbishop Sheen received his greatest accolade when Pope John Paul II embraced him at St. Patrick's Cathedral in New York City. The Holy Father said to him, "You have written and spoken well of the Lord Jesus. You are a loyal son of the Church."

The Good Lord called Fulton Sheen home on December 9, 1979. His television broadcasts, now on tape, and his books continue his earthly work of winning souls for Christ. Sheen's cause for canonization was opened in 2002 and in 2012, Pope Benedict XVI declared him "Venerable." In July of 2019, Pope Francis formally approved the miracle that is attributed to the intercession of the Venerable Archbishop Fulton J. Sheen. This announcement allows a beatification ceremony to take place in the future. The time and date for the church to declare Archbishop Fulton J. Sheen a saint is in God's hands.

Bibliography Notes

(First Meditation) - Fulton J. Sheen, The Seven Last Words – (New York: Century Co. Ltd., 1933), pp. 13-19.

(Second Meditation) - Fulton J. Sheen, The Fullness of Christ – (Huntington, IN: Our Sunday Visitor, 1935), pp. 148-150.

(Third Meditation) - Fulton J. Sheen, Calvary And The Mass – (New York: P.J. Kenedy & Sons, 1936), pp. 29-40.

(Fourth Meditation) - Fulton J. Sheen, The Cross And The Beatitudes, - (New York: P.J. Kenedy & Sons, 1937), pp. 21-35.

(Fifth Meditation) - Fulton J. Sheen, The Rainbow of Sorrow - (New York: P.J. Kenedy & Sons 1938), pp. 20-33.

(Sixth Meditation) - Fulton J. Sheen, Victory Over Vice – (New York: P.J. Kenedy & Sons, 1939), pp. 14-26.

(Seventh Meditation) - Fulton J. Sheen, The Seven Virtues - (New York: P.J. Kenedy & Sons, 1940), pp. 26-42.

(Eighth Meditation) - Fulton J. Sheen, Seven Words To The Cross – (New York: P.J. Kenedy & Sons, 1944), pp. 25-37.

(Ninth Meditation) - Fulton J. Sheen, Seven Words of Jesus and Mary - (New York: P.J. Kenedy & Sons, 1945), pp. 33-45.

On The Front Cover

Jesus and the Thieves

–

A Painting by Michael O'Brien (2008)

Artist Commentary: Jesus promises Paradise to the repentant thief. We tend to think that when severe trials come we will suffer with the same courage and love as Jesus did. Or, perhaps as the "good thief" did. Yet we often find ourselves reacting to trials in the manner of the unrepentant thief. Within our hearts is the potential for all three responses. In life's difficulties we are refined and tested, our hearts are revealed to us, that we might turn and turn again to the One who died for us on the Cross. If we do not succumb to bitterness or despair, or run from what we must learn, we will be with Him "this day in Paradise."

Books Available Through
Bishop Sheen Today Publishing

The Rainbow of Sorrow

The Seven Last Words

Calvary and the Mass

Love One Another

The Cross and the Beatitudes

The Cross and the Crisis

Love One Another

Victory Over Vice

The Seven Virtues

For God and Country

God and War

The Divine Verdict

God Love You

The Seven Last Words Explained

The Priest Is Not His Own

The Cross and the Crib

Philosophies at War

The Seven Last Words of Christ Explained

Father, Forgive Them for They Know Not What They Do.

This Day Thou Shall Be with Me in Paradise

Woman Behold Your Son; Behold Your Mother

My God! My God! Why Hast Thou Forsaken Me?

I Thirst

It is Finished

Father Into Your Hands I Commend My Spirit

Liberty, Equality and Fraternity

Missions and the World Crisis

Seven Words to the Cross

Seven Pillars of Peace

The Holy Hour Prayer Book

Seven Words of Jesus & Mary

www.bishopsheentoday.com

www.ingramcontent.com/pod-product-compliance
Lightning Source LLC
Chambersburg PA
CBHW021648120626
46545CB00002B/749